WEDDING
RECEPTIONS

WEDDING RECEPTIONS

Arranging a Joyous Celebration

JO PACKHAM

A Sterling/Chapelle Book

Sterling Publishing Co., Inc. New York

Jo Packham / Author

Tina Annette Brady / Designer
Cherie Hanson / Editor
Margaret Shields Marti / Executive Editor

Library of Congress Cataloging-in-Publication Data

Packham, Jo.
    Wedding receptions : arranging a joyous celebration / by Jo Packham
        p.   cm.
    "A Sterling/Chapelle book."
    Includes index.
    ISBN 0-8069-8833-9
    1. Weddings—Planning.   2. Wedding etiquette.   I. Title.
    HQ745.P3555   1993   93-25⁹
    395' .22—dc20   CIP

10 9 8 7 6 5 4 3 2 1

A Sterling/Chapelle Book

Published by Sterling Publishing Company, Inc.
387 Park Avenue South, New York, N.Y. 10016
© 1993 by Chapelle Ltd.
Distributed in Canada by Sterling Publishing
$^c/_o$ Canadian Manda Group, P.O. Box 920, Station U
Toronto, Ontario, Canada M8Z 5P9
Distributed in Great Britain and Europe by Cassell PLC
Villiers House, 41/47 Strand, London WC2N 5JE, England
Distributed in Australia by Capricorn Link Ltd.
P.O. Box 665, Lane Cove, NSW 2066
Manufactured in the United States of America

Sterling ISBN 0-8069-8833-9

Contents

Introduction

Congratulations! Yesterday you were single and in love; today you are engaged and a blushing bride-to-be! You are most certainly feeling the emotions that brides have felt for hundreds of years—excited, nervous, overwhelmed, and anxious. Anxious to begin making plans that will lead to the most beautiful wedding you can imagine. Anxious to find a ceremony site. Anxious to call the baker and order the cake. Anxious to plan a reception that will be shared with and remembered always by family and friends.

Some anxiety is normal, but thorough and careful planning will lead to the end result that you so desire. Whether you are orchestrating a large, formal affair for 500 or conducting a small garden ceremony and reception intended to be shared only with those closest to you, you will need to make decisions about style, location, flowers, the wedding cake and much, much more.

Reception Style

The decisions you make between "yes" and "I do" will mostly concern the reception. The reception is usually the event that is shared by the largest number of guests and is the memorable finale to one of the most important days of your life.

One of the first decisions you will make concerns the style of the reception you will be having. Will it be formal and very traditional? Will it follow an informal, contemporary theme such as a western barbecue? Will it be somewhere in between? What follow are some brief descriptions for reception styles and a chart to help give you an overall picture of what each style represents.

Very Formal / Formal

Steeped in tradition and laced with all of the pageantry and finery the occasion has to offer is the formal wedding. The ceremony is eloquent and religious, the wedding party is extensive, the gowns are grand, the men are dressed in tails, limousines deliver you and your father to the church and drive off with the groom and you, his beloved. The reception that follows is truly an event to remember.

A formal reception is large and lavish, usually with a sit-down dinner or a very extensive buffet; it includes champagne and an open bar. There is music for dancing and decorations to admire. The flowers are extraordinary and the wedding cake is a work of art.

Semiformal

Most formal wedding procedures apply to the smaller, semiformal wedding ceremony and reception; they are simply done on a less lavish scale.

You will have fewer guests, the ceremony may or may not be of a religious nature, the wedding party consists of one to three attendants with the same number of groomsmen, and the reception can be beautiful but less ostentatious.

A semiformal reception usually offers a light buffet with champagne and selected other beverages available. Sometimes there is music to dance to and decorations that are less elaborate. The flowers are usually kept to a minimum and the wedding cake is more traditional. The semiformal reception is as lovely as the very formal affair in a smaller, simpler way.

Informal

An intimate, informal wedding event may be held anywhere from a small chapel to your home. Guests are welcomed and directed by a member of the wedding party who is familiar with almost everyone invited. You are dressed in a lovely dress and the groom is sporting a business suit; the two of you will mingle with the guests before the ceremony.

The informal reception may be very small and simple. A dessert buffet may be offered with coffees and wine. There are seldom more than 50 guests, an honor attendant for both you and the groom, and a small symbolic wedding cake.

Traditional

The traditional wedding reception usually follows a religious ceremony held in a church or a civil ceremony performed on the premises. It may be held in a reception center, a hotel, your home, or another "expected" type of wedding establishment.

At the traditional reception you will find all of the events you expect: a receiving line, traditional toasts to you and the groom, a cutting of the cake ceremony, the throwing of the bouquet, dancing, and the traditional departure with the throwing of rice.

Nontraditional

Some couples think the taking of vows in a church or hotel with any type of traditional reception to follow is entirely too mainstream for their wants or needs. They prefer an event that is associated with what they love to do together the most. Those who love to ski can be married on the slopes with a party to follow in

Who Pays for What
_____ at the Reception _____

You and your family, traditionally, pay for such items as the reception music, guest book, catering charges, all food and beverages, flowers and decorations for the reception site, gratuities and other services such as security, transportation of the bridal party to the reception site, photographer and photographs, the wedding cake or cakes, and rental fee for the reception site. The groom and/or his family pay for your going-away corsage and throwing bouquet.

Today, because many couples are older, because they choose to live together first, or are marrying for the second time, they ʊ﹁ ↴o finance the entire wedding themselves. In this situation, the families help in a small way, such as paying for the rehearsal dinner or perhaps the flowers. If you and the groom have decided to finance the wedding yourselves, the two of you will need to decide how much and which one of you will pay for what. You might divide the costs directly down the middle or divide them down more traditional lines with you taking your family's responsibilities and the groom taking his. (For an entire list of wedding expenses, see *Wedding Attendants* by Jo Packham.)

An additional option the two of you may want to discuss with both families is a three-way split between you and the groom, your parents and the groom's parents. Another division is to pay for the number of guests each invites. If the groom's family does help to pay for the festivities, they become co-hosts with your parents.

—— *Your Budget* ——

Once you have decided between the two of you who will finance the festivities and then spoken to other family members about their financial contribution, you can begin to plan your wedding. The planning begins with setting your priorities. First, decide what it is that you care about the most in regard to the wedding. For some, it is the food and, for other couples, it may be the entertainment or the flowers. After prioritizing each component, you need to carefully prepare your budget and promise yourselves to adhere to that budget. It is so easy to add $100 here and $100 there and pretty soon you have doubled the amount you had first estimated.

Begin your budgeting process by taking the monies that are available and devising a budget by category that will set the limits of how much can be spent in each category, such as the photographer, the cake, the caterer and so on.

Adapt the following checklist to your needs, and make certain you use it whenever you are meeting with someone who is providing something for the reception. This checklist is simply a general overall guideline so that you can see total expenditures in each category. You will want to have detailed and complete checklists from which to work for each category.

❖ **To avoid overpaying and to insure you are getting the best price for the best product from the best company, you may want to follow some of the suggestions below:**

1. Become familiar with the terminology used and the requirements for everything that has to do with weddings. If you know what you are asking for or about, if you are familiar with the terminology and what is involved, then it is less likely that you will be taken advantage of or end up paying for something you do not actually need or want. For example, when ordering stationery items, you need to know the weights of paper, the difference between engraving and offset printing, and which enclosure cards are necessary for your style and formality of ceremony and reception.

2. Do comparison shopping. The desire to eliminate comparison shopping is very understandable because there is so much to do and so little time. If you take the time to contact three establishments in regard to each budgeted item, you will be fairly certain of understanding the market price and that you are getting a good price for a product or services rendered.

   To help with your comparison shopping, you may want to ask each person contacted for a minimum of two references, a list of specific policies, and his/her price on a specific item. For example, three estimates on a specific item, such as a corsage for your mother that has a single pink rose surrounded by baby's breath, would be a helpful measure.

3. Be assertive but not unreasonable. You are often so overwhelmed with what needs to be done and so unfamiliar with what you are ordering and arranging for that it is easy to be intimidated and forget you are the employer and the people who are being hired are the employees. Remember, it is your wedding and if you want something done differently than the way they usually handle the situation, you have a right to insist or take your business elsewhere.

4. Always inquire about quantity discounts. If you are ordering all of your flowers from one florist, for example, you should not have to pay the same price for each dozen roses used as a person who is ordering only one dozen for Mother's Day.

5. Read the contracts carefully. Contracts are meant to list responsibilities and to protect both you and the retailer from miscommunication. For more information about contracts, see page 23.

6. Choose alteration or delivery dates that are as far in the future as is reasonable for the item being ordered. This will allow as much time as possible to make changes if the items are unacceptable. For example, the

delivery date on your dress could be months or weeks before the wedding date, which would allow you to have it altered or order another if there are problems with the one delivered.

7. Pay as small a deposit as possible and use your credit card. This may be the best way to protect yourself when paying for items or services rendered. If you put the initial deposit on your credit card and then the supplier fails to adhere to his agreements in the contract, you have some recourse through the credit card company.

8. Here are some hints for saving money on your reception

• Plan your reception for morning or early afternoon. Brunch is less expensive than dinner. At an afternoon reception you could serve hors d'oeuvres or have a dessert buffet with white wine and/or soft drinks.

• Look for less expensive sites, such as someone's home, church meeting halls, community centers, or parks.

• Borrow, rather than rent, the extra equipment that you may need.

• Have friends and family make some or all of the food. Do not have a cocktail hour or an open bar.

- Use flowers that are in season, pick flowers from friends' and families' gardens or use potted plants. Another alternative is to rent the flowers you need and then use the same flowers to decorate both the ceremony and reception sites.

- Find an alternative to a band such as hiring a disc jockey with tapes, have friends provide the music, or hire musicians for a minimum amount of time.

- Hire a professional photographer to take only certain pictures of the reception, and then have family and friends take the remainder of the photographs.

- Ask family and friends to help with the serving, bartending, and the cleanup.

The best way to pay for a lovely moment is to enjoy it.
Richard Bach

Contracts

Contracts can be a very important part of your wedding plans and are intended to protect both you and the retailer from miscommunication. Each contract, regardless of the form it takes, should include both parties' responsibilities as well as the following:

- All dates and times, such as when an order was placed, when it is to be delivered and other details

- Name and phone number of the person responsible and in charge of the order

- All details about every item ordered

- An itemized list of all goods and services to be provided, such as the number of people enlisted to help, what services are to be performed, what hours they are required to stay, and what equipment they are to supply

- Individual and total costs for all items or services

- Delivery time schedule

- Backup services available

- Payment schedule

- Specified date to give final head count to caterer, reception hall and others; cancellation policy (including last date to make changes and charges)

- Signatures of both buyer and seller

- Guarantee of services or a refund (For example, if you hire a photographer and the pictures come out poorly through no fault of your own, then you owe him nothing and are entitled to a refund of your deposit.)

❖ **You should have contracts with every person or establishment that is providing each product or service. For example, contracts should be signed with the following:**

- The shops that are supplying the wedding attire

- The stationer

- The wedding coordinator

- The reception site (which may include everything, some things, or simply the building)

- Any additional rental companies that are supplying equipment

- The baker

- The caterer (if not included in reception site)

- The florist

- The musicians

- The photographer and videographer

- The limousine company

- Any additional persons supplying manpower or services

Planning
the Reception

After you and the groom have decided upon the style of your wedding and have agreed on the financing and budget for the entire affair, you can begin the planning of your festivities. Careful and detailed planning can insure the "perfect" wedding. If you are planning a small affair with fewer than a hundred guests, you, your immediate family, and attendants can probably do all of the planning yourselves. If you intend to have a large, formal affair, you will need professional help, probably from a wedding coordinator.

Remember to include the groom in any major decisions concerning the wedding festivities. Getting his advice can not only be a major help but can also make him feel involved and can get your marriage off on a positive note of communicating and sharing.

Setting the Date

The next step, after selecting the style and determining the financing and the budget, in planning your reception is to select a date and time for the wedding festivities. If you opt for a holiday or holiday weekend, you will need to allow additional time between the making of reservations for the actual site and all other arrangements and the agreed upon date, since everyone is booked far in advance for busy holiday times. If you choose a less popular date, you will not have to worry quite so much about the lead time in making reservations. Every season will have its advantages and disadvantages. If you choose to have a beautiful Christmas wedding, the weather may make it difficult for transportation; during the summer several of the guests may have vacations planned and may be unable to change their arrangements.

You will probably wish to begin by selecting several dates because there are so many sites, services, and people who need to be available on the date selected that you may find your first choice is simply impossible.

Selecting a Time

Next, consider the time of day for your reception. Your choice may be determined by your religious beliefs, by the availability of the site, by the formality of the occasion, and by where you live. In the West, evening receptions are most popular while, in the Southwest, afternoon celebrations are most common. Both afternoon and evening weddings are better attended if held on a Saturday or a Sunday. Ideally, and to insure attendance, the reception should immediately follow the ceremony.

❖ **The time of your reception dictates, to a certain extent, what type of reception it will be. The traditional types are listed below.**

Morning

Breakfast or brunch: A breakfast or brunch reception is most acceptable following a morning wedding at 9 or 10 a.m. This may be served either buffet-style or as a sit-down meal. Champagne, wine, mixed morning drinks, or coffee and juices are most often served. You may or may not choose to serve your wedding cake. Alternatives are to have small cakes made and put into bakery boxes or simply have your cake cut and put in small boxes for guests to take home.

Afternoon

Luncheon: This reception is similar to a brunch and may be either buffet-style or a sit-down affair. A luncheon reception usually follows a late morning or high noon ceremony and occurs between 12 and 2 p.m.

Tea: A tea reception is usually held between 2 and 5 p.m., with coffee, tea, punch, wine, or soft drinks, and champagne for toasting you and the groom. You may elect to serve a dessert buffet or traditional "tea"-type finger foods. You will almost always cut your wedding cake at this affair.

Cocktail: A cocktail reception occurs between the hours of 4 and 7:30 p.m. Usually champagne, wine, cocktails, or soft drinks are served. You may offer hors d'oeuvres, or a light buffet of only finger foods. Again, you will almost always elect to cut your cake.

Evening

Dessert: It is appropriate, in some parts of the country, to only serve cake and beverages at the evening reception. The beverages are usually limited in nature and served with the dessert. Usually you serve your cake as part of the dessert.

Dinner or Buffet: This is the most traditional type of reception. It usually takes place from 7 p.m. to 10 p.m. or later. There is almost always a fairly extensive buffet or a more formal sit-down dinner. There may or may not be an open bar, but all types of beverages are served. You will always elect to cut the cake and have it served for dessert.

The Guest List

Another step in planning your reception is deciding upon the number of guests on your list. As a general rule, 75% of those invited will actually attend if it is on a weekend or over a holiday; if it takes place during the week or during the summer months, 60% attendance is probably more realistic. There are several considerations when arriving at a number for your guest list:

Your wedding style—a formal, traditional-style wedding usually dictates a larger guest list than an informal wedding style.

Your budget—how many can you realistically afford to invite?

Yours, the groom's, and both families wishes on how many to include on the guest list—you and the groom will need to decide how many you would like to invite for the style of wedding you are dreaming of. You will then need to talk to both families and come to a joint decision on who will invite how many and who will pay for those on the list. Ideally, all invited guests attend both the ceremony and the reception. There are several ways of deciding how many each member will invite; therefore, it is important that everyone involved agree and feel good about the final decision.

Your location—how many will the reception site actually accommodate?

Your wedding participants' spouses, escorts and families—You must always invite the wedding officiant and spouse, the wedding party and spouses or dates, and the parents of child attendants. You may also wish to include the parents of your wedding party if you know them well. You should include all guests who were invited to the engagement party and any showers or parties that were given in your honor.

Your decision on whether or not and how many special guests to include—these are persons who have grown up with you or the groom or work with either family, such as baby-sitters, housekeepers, caretakers, and others.

Your policy for inviting children—should they or should they not be included? If there are only a few children you wish to include, perhaps they could become part of the wedding party. If not, you could invite them by sending them their own invitation. Remember, however, to be considerate of everyone's feelings. If some guests have been asked not to bring their children and arrive to see other guests' children, they may be uncomfortable with the situation. Remember that children quickly fill the number of names allowed for your list.

Choosing the
———— Reception Site ————

Selecting a location for the occasion is next. Local visitors' bureaus may have a guide to area facilities that are available for receptions. Your local chamber of commerce or historical society office may have additional leads. Community park departments will know the availability, requirements, and restrictions for public sites often used for wedding receptions.

Begin your search for a reception site as soon as you have selected the date for your wedding. Prime dates can be booked up to a year in advance. Popular months for weddings vary by regions: December in the South, Valentine's Day everywhere, and weekends in June are almost impossible to book on either coast. Be aware that religious restrictions may rule out certain days or times of the year. For example, Catholics and Greek Orthodox avoid marrying during Lent in March and Jews do not have weddings during the High Holy Days (usually in September and October).

When you plan the location, keep in mind the preparations you may have to orchestrate. Consider all of the details, including how accessible the site is, what facilities exist for guest parking and seating, and what equipment is available.

If it is outdoors, remember to select a quiet spot that is away from the traffic. It would be wise to select an alternate location in case the weather is bad. Visit the site at the same time of day that your reception is planned to make certain the lighting is appropriate for the style of wedding and the activities you have planned.

For any facility, check on all restrictions that are imposed regardless of whether the location is inside or outside. Is there a limitation on the number of guests? Are there fire restrictions prohibiting candles? Are there liability precautions prohibiting the throwing of rice or rose petals? Are there sound restrictions on music? Do they have facilities for handicapped guests? What outside services are you allowed to use?

Reception Sites

Hotel/Club /Restaurant

Consider all possibilities for the atmosphere, room size, and price range that suit your style, your needs, and your wants the best. There is often no charge for site rental if the establishment caters the reception—although this option is not always as cost effective as it sounds.

❖ **These establishments usually have a variety of "wedding packages," depending on the date and style of your reception. When selecting a site like this, the following questions may be helpful:**

• Is a wedding package offered?

• If so, what exactly is included and what is the total cost?

• Is there a guarantee requirement for number of guests?

• When must the final guest count be delivered?

• What does the actual site look like? Is the site to be shared with another wedding or event? If so, how is it to be divided? How is privacy and timing of events (like food delivery) insured?

• Is it permissible to make any substitutions in any of the arrangements? Is there a charge?

• Is there an appropriate place for a receiving line?

• What drinks are served? How is the cost for the drinks calculated? When are they served? Is there a refund for drinks not used? If there is liquor, will it be brand names? Is the bartender included?

- Are there arrangements for a head table?

- What food is served? How is the amount of food calculated? What is the staff-to-guest ratio? (For seated meals, the ratio should be one waiter per eight to ten guests.) Is there a set menu or can a selection be made from a variety of items? If a sit-down meal is decided upon, are all guests served the same items? Can substitutions be made? Can there be special considerations for guests who require special dietary restrictions? May you sample the food you select beforehand? Can you see how another similar package is set up?

- What does a place setting look like and consist of? Do you have a choice of linens and colors?

- Do they supply the wedding cake? Are you required to select one of their styles? How much does it cost?

- Are there additional decorations and what do they look like?

- Do they have a florist or do you provide your own?

- Is extra equipment available, such as a gift table and guest book table? Is there an additional charge?

- Are the rental hours for the site set or can the hours be extended or open? How early can you arrive and how late can you leave? Is there an additional fee?

- Are all taxes and gratuities covered in the cost?

- Are there additional charges for required services, such as security guards, coat check, parking attendants, and doormen?

- Is there insurance against breakage or damage?

- What deposits are required and when?

- What is their policy on cancellations?

Reception Centers

All questions and considerations for a hotel, club or restaurant apply here also.

Home Reception

Traditionally your parents' home was the only choice, although now it has become acceptable for the home of a close friend, a relative, or the groom's family to provide the perfect setting for your reception. You must remember, however, that to have a large wedding in a home is indeed entertaining on a grand scale and the preparation may be more than you anticipate. Organization and delegation of responsibilities are essential. Consider hiring a wedding coordinator to handle all of the arrangements so that nothing will be overlooked, and so you and the hostess will be free to enjoy yourselves before and during the festivities. You can probably rent everything you need from a rental agency or borrow the items from family and friends.

If your reception at home is to include more than 30 people, you will definitely need the help of a caterer. The caterer may provide any of the following: food, beverages, the wedding cake, the serving staff, crystal and china, tables and chairs, and some will provide tents, dance floors, and innumerable other services.

When using a caterer, regardless of the location, be certain that every service to be provided for and the total itemized costs are given to you in a contract. As with all contracts, make certain you read it carefully, understanding every word. Have a third party read it with you to catch anything you may have missed. Be sure that you are in agreement with all costs and terms.

❖ **The following points, specifically, should be covered in your contract with the caterer:**

- Detailed menu—cost per serving; how and when it will be served

- List of beverages—how they will be served and charged for; are there refunds for unopened bottles?

- Wedding cake(s)

- Number of serving staff

- Gratuities

- Number of tables and chairs—when they will be set up and taken down

- Delivery charges

- Overtime charges

- Coat check facilities and charges

- Tents or marquees

- Insurance against breakage

- Are taxes included?

- Deposits

Outdoor Reception

A large garden or park is a perfect place for an outdoor reception that ranges from formal to informal. If you are certain you desire an outdoor wedding reception but do not know the best place, try consulting the chamber of commerce, private clubs, historic sites, private estates, or parks departments. Contact the person in charge of the location and discuss all details with him/her. Sign a contract that specifies all aspects of renting or using the location: arrival times, departure times, equipment that can be used, cleanup responsibilities, parking facility use, and others. Make certain that you have arranged deposits and fees.

If possible, spend the same day of the week at the same hours the reception will take place to thoroughly familiarize yourself with the daily traffic and other obstacles. Be aware of the time of day and the temperature. You do not want guests to be eating in the hot sun or the cake to be placed where it could melt or have leaves falling on it.

Make a map and mail it to guests so they will know how to get there. You will be wise to arrange for alternate sites in case of bad weather. You might even enclose a small card with the invitation, giving this kind of information: "In the event of inclement weather, the wedding will be held at—." Or you may want to arrange for large party tents to ensure that the reception goes off no matter what.

offer advice and resources. Any bride can use the services of a wedding coordinator if she feels it would aid in making the event run smoothly and on budget.

On the other hand, you may have an experienced friend whose help and guidance is exactly what you need to coordinate the details for your wedding. Combined with your own skills and experience, the two of you may choose to divide the tasks in the checklist rather than use a professional coordinator.

❖ Below are certain situations in which coordinators are particularly helpful:

- Very large formal weddings and receptions

- Weddings where you are too busy, due to work agendas or other situations, to see to your own wedding plans

- An at-home wedding which requires special and all services

- Weddings being held far from where you are living

- Long weekend or progressive weddings where schedules and services need to be coordinated

❖ **A good wedding coordinator can be located by one of the following methods:**

- Ask family and friends for any recommendations.

- Ask other wedding professionals (bridal salon personnel, caterers, or florists) whom they might recommend.

- Look in the Yellow Pages under Wedding Consultants.

❖ **When you select your coordinator, follow these suggestions:**

1. Choose two or three coordinators from the sources listed above. Make an appointment with each and allow one to two hours to discuss the details.

   Do not confuse a wedding coordinator with an independent consultant that you would find employed in a wedding-related store, such as a bridal consultant in the wedding shop where you purchased your gown. Such consultants are in-house employees who specialize in helping with only one item or service on your wedding list and are paid by the establishment where they work.

2. Inquire as to the services they provide and a general fee for each service rendered.

Some coordinator's fees are an agreed upon flat fee; some charge a per-guest rate; some charge a per-hour fee; others may charge a percentage of the total wedding costs, usually 15% to 20%. It is an accepted practice for the coordinator to also make a commission from the outside services he/she uses.

3. Ask for names of suppliers he/she has worked with and a minimum of three recommendations from other brides whose weddings he/she has coordinated. Be certain to personally contact each reference.

4. Discuss your ideas but keep an open mind, being flexible and receptive; the consultant may have several good ideas to add to your own.

5. Give the coordinator all of the facts you have decided upon to date concerning the wedding and the reception.
    a. Style of wedding you prefer
    b. Ceremony and reception sites
    c. Time of day
    d. Your budget

6. Look at albums depicting the receptions the consultant has personally arranged.

7. Ask for suggestions and estimates within your budget.

8. Find out how many weddings the consultant books in one time period. If he/she books too heavily, chances are you will

not receive the attention to details that are so important.

9. Find out exactly which items and services he/she is responsible for and which you must provide yourself.

10. Make certain that the person you speak with is the one who will be in charge of the details for your wedding and that he/she will not turn your actual work over to a less-experienced employee.

11. Make certain that he/she will attend the rehearsal, the ceremony, and the reception in person to guarantee that all will run smoothly and according to plan.

12. Give your coordinator a checklist to work from that not only lists all of the above information but all of the details necessary in each category. In addition, the checklist should include the names and telephone numbers of everyone in the wedding party, all persons in charge of services that the coordinator is not handling, and a detailed list of all duties you see the coordinator overseeing.

Catering

The wedding reception has an enormous series of services and details that need to be negotiated and attended to. Food and drink, the largest portions of the budget, can be handled several different ways. If you have selected a site that includes these in the rental package, you need only go over the details. If you are having a small, informal home wedding, friends and family may be enlisted to cook and serve, as well as act as bartender. If you are having an outdoor wedding or a large, formal wedding in a location that does not provide for food and drink, you will need to hire the services of a caterer.

Selecting a Caterer

A caterer may be an individual who is a fine cook and prepares food for small parties of ten to 60. A large, professional catering service may have mobile kitchens, prepare the meal, serve it, and provide everything that is needed in conjunction with it, such as reception decorations, linens, china, crystal, serving dishes, and tables. Some even supply the parking attendants.

How does one find a caterer? To find a good caterer, you may follow the same suggestions as listed on page 48 for locating a competent wedding coordinator.

❖ **After you have selected a caterer, you may want to follow some of these suggestions:**

1. Choose two or three caterers. Make an appointment with each, allowing one to two hours to discuss the details.

2. Discuss your ideas but keep an open mind and be flexible and receptive; the caterer may have several ideas to add to your own.

   A good caterer will welcome your suggestions and help you develop your wedding reception menu so that it incorporates the best of a combination of ideas and reflects your tastes and personality.

3. Give the caterer a menu and a list of beverages that you have in mind that is indicative of the style of food/beverage you wish to have served.

4. Give the caterer all of the facts concerning the wedding reception that will help in his/her determinations:
   a. Style of reception
   b. Reception site

c. Time of day
d. Estimated number of guests
e. Budget allocated to catering

5. Look at menus and albums of events that he/she has personally catered. If he/she is as good as he/she should be, several original recipes will be suggested and/or the caterer will be willing to use yours, keeping them confidential. Find out if the season will affect the availability of items you have requested. Find out how the caterer calculates how much food is needed. Make certain that you can taste all items several weeks before the reception so that if something is unsatisfactory, it can be eliminated from the menu and replaced with another item.

6. Discuss all options in regard to beverage service. How are you to be charged if there is an open bar? What hours will the bartender be available and how is he/she paid? Is there a corkage fee? How will the champagne for the toasting be served? What is done with unopened bottles? How is the quantity for different beverages calculated?

7. Ask for additional suggestions and estimates for both food and drink within your budget.

8. Find out if the caterer is capable of supplying you with bonded, trained chefs and waiters, waitresses, and bartenders.

9. Find out which services the caterer provides and if there are additional charges, such as for setup, the actual servers' or bartender's time, and the cleanup.

10. Find out how many weddings or events the caterer will schedule in one day. If over-booked, he/she will not be able to give you the quality you are looking for.

11. Find out how much advance time the caterer will need to set up and the estimated time to dismantle everything. Are these charges included or extra?

❖ **On the average, the following guidelines are used for calculating beverages:**

One bottle of wine = six to eight partially filled glasses

One quart of hard liquor = twenty 1½-oz drinks

One 26-oz bottle of champagne = eight servings

½ keg of beer = 260 8-oz glasses

One 26-oz bottle of juice/soft drink = eight servings

12. Find out exactly how the food will be arranged and served. Will there be chefs strategically located to cut the beef or serve certain entrees? Will the waiters serve additional drinks while guests are in the receiving line or are seated at the table?

13. Find out exactly which rental items the caterer supplies and if there are additional charges for each of these items. Some may be included in the price of the food or beverage and some may not.

14. Find out if the caterer is willing to free you from all responsibilities before, during, and after the reception.

15. Find out what is done with the leftover food and drink. Do they provide containers to store it in? You are paying for it, so family members might as well take it home. Will the caterer take back unopened liquor and soft drink bottles and not charge you for them?

16. Make certain that the caterer you speak with is the one who will be in charge of the actual preparation and the service at the reception and that he/she will not turn the work over to a less-experienced employee.

17. Make certain that the contract you sign clearly and completely lists all foods, beverages, equipment, services, and delivery times. Also, make certain that all costs are calculated, explained, and clearly identified. Here, more than any other place, it is mandatory that everything be written down and clearly understood by all parties concerned.

Real joy, believe me, is a serious matter.

Seneca

Catering Your Own Wedding

If you are having a small, informal wedding consisting of fewer than 50 guests, catering the affair yourself is a reasonable task.

❖ **You will want to consider the following recommendations when catering your own reception:**

1. Plan your menu so that the shopping can be completed and the items can be prepared weeks in advance or arrange with family and friends to prepare and deliver the meal immediately before the reception. Plan a menu with recipes you have personally tested. You do not want to give a recipe to the person making it and then find out that it is unclear or that an ingredient has been left out.

   To be certain the items can be frozen, you will need to make a batch of each item ahead of time, freeze it, and then thaw it to make certain it maintains its quality.

   Arrange to have family and friends freeze the prepared items for you. It is probably not possible to store all items yourself.

2. Calculate the amount of liquor you will need and order it ahead of time. Order more than you will need, but make certain the store will take back any unopened bottles

and give you a refund. An average guest will drink between two to five drinks at the reception. To help with your beverage calculations, see page 60.

3. Make certain there is enough food and that the bar is well stocked. You do not want to run out before everyone is served.

4. Solicit the help of family and friends to serve and tend bar or hire the minimum services of professionals. They should be instructed what to wear, shown all of the facilities, given a list of what is to be served, and given a timetable of events.

5. Organize your helpers. Put someone who is dependable and organized in charge of the person preparing and serving. Make lists of who is to prepare what, when it is to be delivered, and duties that are to be performed. Then give a complete list to the person in charge and individual lists to each helper so everyone is clear about what is to be done and when.

6. Order your serving dishes and other necessary equipment from a party rental shop or ask to borrow from family and friends. This should be done two to three months ahead of time to make certain you will have everything that is needed. Check to see if the rental store has delivery service. If you are using borrowed pieces, ask for them to be delivered several days before the wedding. Make certain each borrowed piece

has the owner's name, address, and phone number taped on the bottom.

7. Set up the food tables and the bar at least four hours ahead of time. The dining tables should also be set up at this time, if they will not be in the way of the ceremony.

8. Servers who are not helping set up should arrive approximately one hour early so they can become acquainted with the area and their duties.

9. Make certain you discuss a fee with each helper. If they are friends and family who are donating their time and expertise, make certain you write them a thank-you note and give each a gift at the end of the reception.

10. You will want to prepare a complete checklist for the person in charge, including the above material as well as the names of key participants, the reception site, the time of all events, the names and numbers of all catering helpers, a list of all food, beverages, supplies and anything else that is pertinent to completion of his/her job.

11. You will also want to prepare individual checklists for each helper, adapting the information to what is necessary for each to know. This way no one will have questions as to what is expected and when.

CATERING CHECKLIST

Organization is the key to a smooth reception whether you cater the food or a professional does it. Adapt this checklist to meet your needs.

Name of Person in Charge/Caterer_____

Address_____

Phone_____

Menu_____

_____

_____

_____

_____

Price per Person_____

Gratuities_____

Taxes_____

Beverages_____

_____

_____

_____

_____

Corkage Fee_____

Unopened Bottles_____

Bartender_____

Servers_____

Equipment Needed:

Linens_____ _____

Obtained From_____

Delivery Date_____

Glassware_____ _____

Obtained From_____ _____

Delivery Date_____ _____ _____

Silverware_____

Obtained From_____

Delivery Date_____

China_____

Obtained From_____

Delivery Date_____ _____

Serving Dishes_____

Obtained From_____ _____

Delivery Date_____

Tables_____

Obtained From_____

Delivery Date and Time_____

Chairs_____

Obtained From_____

Delivery Date and Time_____

Breakdown of Price:

Food Total_____

Beverage Total_____

Services_____

Personnel_____

Equipment_____

Additional Charges_____

Cleanup Charges_____

Overtime Charges_____

Balance Due Date_____

Cancellation Policy_____

Total Due_____

CATERING YOUR OWN WEDDING

Person Shopping for Food_____

Phone_____

Food Delivered to Each Person on

_____

Persons to Deliver Food to_____

_____

_____

_____

Person Shopping for Beverages_____

Phone_____

Beverages Delivery Date and Time_____

Persons Preparing Food:

Name_____

Phone_____

Item_____

Delivery Date and Time_____

Name_____

Phone_____

Item_____

Delivery Date and Time_____

The Wedding Cake

One of the strongest traditions associated with your wedding is the wedding cake. Its shape, flavor, and decorations are dictated by personal taste and by the style of wedding you have selected. The size will be determined by the number of guests it will be serving.

You should order your cake three months before the wedding (even earlier if it is a busy season). You can order your cake from the caterer, a local reputable bakery, an individual that you are certain can create the cake you have in mind, or from the reception site (if it is a hotel or reception center).

You will want to shop for bakers the same way you shopped for a wedding coordinator or a caterer (see page 48). You will also want to interview at least three so that you can compare quality, originality, and price. It is important to discuss the decorations on the wedding cake in great detail. You want to make certain that the baker "sees" what you see. Pictures of cakes you have seen in magazines or the baker's own portfolio may be of help in this situation. If you dream of having a "garden of cabbage roses" adorn your cake, you will be most disappointed if your cake is delivered and there are traditional frosting roses scattered around. You will also want to taste the cake and icing flavors you choose before yours is made. Chocolate cake with raspberry filling may sound perfect, when in reality, it is too sweet for the time of day of your reception. The baker can help with which cakes, flavorings, and decorations can travel well, hold up in the heat of an outdoor wedding, or other considerations. Make certain that you discuss size and price with the baker as well. A cake can be a very expensive proposition and you do not want any surprises when it is delivered.

Prices for your cake are determined by size and decoration. You may want to select a special flavoring or add your own special decorations to the cake. For example, wedding cakes sometimes include pillars to divide the layers. Instead of using the standard white ones, why not paint them to resemble marble? Or you may wish to decorate your cake with fresh flowers in place of frosting ones. (This should be handled by the florist, not the baker.)

The cake is traditionally topped with some type of ornament. It may be a special floral arrangement, a porcelain bride and groom, or crystal wedding bells. The top decoration is often saved as a keepsake. The top layer is sometimes saved as well. It can be frozen and eaten on your first anniversary or made from cardboard so that it can be removed and placed under a glass dome.

Tradition has it that a piece of the bride's cake (or the groom's cake) under a single woman's pillow will lead her to dream of her future husband. This is why it is customary to cut the cake and serve it at the reception, with extra slices from the next to the top layer provided for guests to take home packed in small boxes.

You might also have a groom's cake, which traditionally was sliced at the end of the reception and boxed in engraved white boxes with your and the groom's initials in silver, and given to guests as favors. The traditional groom's cake was a dark, rich fruitcake with icing. Due to the additional expense of such a cake, today most groom's cakes are the groom's favorite cake and icing. It is cut into individual pieces which are wrapped in paper to match the theme of the wedding and tied with a bow. They are then given to guests to take home.

You will want to draw special attention to your cake by setting it off by itself on a decorated cake table. You may also include an engraved cake knife and server that have been tied with ribbons and/or adorned with tiny fresh or silk flowers to display with your cake.

A beautiful thing is never perfect.

Egyptian folk wisdom

WEDDING CAKE CHECKLIST

Baker/Bakery_____

Address_____

Phone_____

Appointment Date and Time_____

Cake

Size_____

Shape_____

Number of Tiers_____

Number Cake Will Serve_____

Flavor of Cake_____

Flavor of Filling_____

Flavor of Icing/Color_____

Decorations_____

_____

Cake Top_____

Groom's Cake

Size_____

Shape_____

Number Cake Will Serve_____

Flavor of Cake_____

Flavor of Filling_____

Flavor of Icing/Color_____

Decorations_____

Boxes or Wrapping_____

Other_____

_____

_____

Cost_____

_____

Cake Knife_____

Cake Server_____

Cake Table_____

Cake Table Decorations_____

Date and Amount of Deposit_____

Date and Amount of Balance Due_____

Terms of Cancellation_____

Date, Time, Place

of Delivery or Pickup_____

Cost_____

TOTAL COST_____

Reception Flowers ___

Flowers have been the symbol of love and romance throughout the ages. As a bride, your wedding day is probably the most romantic day of your life and the decisions you make concerning your flowers are essential to making it perfect. (For more detailed information on every aspect of flowers for the wedding ceremony and reception and for a detailed checklist from which to work, refer to _Wedding Flowers_ by Jo Packham.)

Flowers are everywhere during a wedding. The bride's flowers include your bouquet, your bouquet for tossing, your going-away corsage, and additional decorative flowers for headpieces or shoes.

The wedding participants' flowers include attendants' bouquets, participants' corsages, groomsmen's boutonnieres, and others.

At the reception site, flowers might be used to decorate the receiving line; the guest book table; table centerpieces including a head table, buffet table, and individual guest tables; champagne toasting glasses; the cake, the cake knife and server, the cake table; and the location where gifts are placed. Flowers can be used to section off a room that is too large, and for additional arrangements as needed.

The flowers you select are somewhat dictated by the style and colors of your wedding, the time of day, the budget you have allocated for flowers, and the season.

You should select your florist as least six months prior to the wedding and make all final arrangements three months prior to the day. If your wedding is during a busy season for florists, the timetable should be nine and six months ahead. You should select your florist the same way you selected your caterer (see page 48.), adding the option of calling Teleflora at (310) 826-5253 and asking for customer service.

❖ When you select your florist, follow these suggestions:

1. Choose two or three florists. Make an appointment with each and allow one hour to discuss the details.

2. Discuss your ideas but keep an open mind, being flexible and receptive; the florist may have several good ideas to add to your own.

3. Give all of the facts concerning the wedding reception:
   a. Style and colors of your wedding
   b. Wedding sites
   c. Time of day

4. Show pictures you have saved from magazines and books that depict the look you want.

5. Look at albums of weddings the florist has personally designed.

6. Ask for suggestions and estimates within your budget.

7. Find out how many weddings the florist will book in one day. If he/she books more than three, chances are this florist is overextended and there may be problems.

8. Find out exactly which rental items the florist supplies and which must be provided by you or the reception site.

9. Find out if the florist charges a delivery or setup fee.

10. Make certain that the florist you speak with will actually be in charge of your flowers (both the designing and the overseeing) and that he/she will not turn the actual work over to a less-experienced employee.

Love is like a rose, the joy of all the earth...

Christina Rossetti

❖ When you have selected the florist, remember the following points:

1. After you have decided definitely which florist to use and before any final decisions on types of arrangements are made, your florist should accompany you to the reception site.

2. The florist should provide sketches of where the flowers will be placed and in what manner they will be displayed, such as in vases, swags, or wreaths.

3. A list of all the flowers you are ordering should be made. If a specific flower is a symbol of your relationship with your fiancé, make certain it is used throughout your arrangements.

4. Make certain the florist has a list of alternate flowers in the event of an unexpected frost or other unanticipated surprise.

5. Make certain your florist has a list of all bouquets, corsages, and arrangements that are needed.

6. If you are having fresh flowers on your cake, make certain that the florist—not the caterer or baker—designs the arrangement.

7. You should provide your florist with the names and telephone numbers of the caterer, wedding coordinator, reception site manager, yourself, and the groom. All but

you and your intended are professionals who should work together to orchestrate your wedding.

8. Determine exactly what time the florist should arrive at the reception site to begin arranging the flowers. This must be coordinated with the site so the florist does not interfere with other events and has enough time to do the arrangements that have been decided upon. Also determine exactly what time the florist should arrive to take down the flowers and where they should be taken.

9. Receive a written contract stating the date, setup and take-down times, place, types of flowers, the number of arrangements, the approximate size the arrangements will be, the total amount of the bill, and the dates required for both the deposit and final payments.

10. Put your deposit on a credit card, which protects you by special consumer protection laws should the florist go out of business before the wedding or fail to stick to the agreements made in the contract.

Where to Decorate

Flowers for the reception may be as extensive as the style of your wedding and your budget will allow. You may select flowers to be used in the following:

Receiving Line

You may opt not to have flowers in the receiving line except those being held by the wedding party, or this may be the place you wish to have a lot of floral arrangements. This is the one place every wedding guest is sure to see because it is customarily where you and the groom will be standing. You can use your imagination here to create any look you want.

Head Table, Guest Tables, Buffet Table, Guest Book Table, and Gift Table

These, again, may range from very formal bouquets in baskets to something as simple as tiny potted pansies. Whichever you select, make certain the table arrangements are low enough so guests can see over the top. Here is another place, however, where you can use your wildest imagination and either make the arrangements yourself or explain these new ideas to your florist.

Wedding Cake Table

The cake table may be decorated to accentuate the beauty of the cake or it may be used to make a simple cake become a work of art. Here, again, use your imagination and do not forget to decorate the knife, the cake server, and the goblets.

Ways to Save Money on Your Wedding Flowers

- Choose a wedding date that is not near a holiday. Demand is so high for flowers at holiday time that the price of flowers naturally increases, popular flowers become scarce and florists have a tendency to overbook their services.

- Select seasonal and regional flowers; avoid exotic flowers.

- Instead of big and expensive bouquets, you might use a single flower.

- Do not overcrowd arrangements. Crowding many flowers into one bouquet lessens the overall impact. Arrangements can be looser and more airy.

- Consider using silk or dried flowers or potted plants. The initial cost may be as expensive as fresh flowers but they can be used as gifts, home or holiday decorations, or reused in a friend's or other family member's wedding.

- Use the same flowers at the ceremony and the reception site.

- Share your floral arrangements with another bride whose reception is shortly before or after yours.

- Rent plants and flower arrangements.

Arranging Your Own Flowers

To keep within your budget, you may elect to arrange your own flowers and not use a professional. You may purchase flowers yourself from several different types of suppliers. After selecting the flowers and the supplier, you will need to turn your attention to the logistics of the day itself. Calculate the number of flowers you will need and place your order two weeks before the event, at which time the supplier should tell you the availability of the flowers requested, the cost of the flowers, and when the flowers can be picked up or delivered.

When you actually start the arrangements depends on the weather, the timetable of events, how much help is available, and the location of the reception. If possible, and if time permits, flowers should be arranged the morning of the wedding. If the timing is too close, flowers may be arranged the day before but should be placed in water and a cool place until they are actually needed.

If professionals are not being used, you will need to carefully select helpers whom you can trust to do the job you want done. For perfect results, work from checklists which identify people, times, tasks and equipment.

—Reception Decorations —

Additional decorations for the reception may be extensive or nonexistent. Some couples feel comfortable with natural surroundings providing the backdrop and decorations; other couples who are being married in a place that is meant for other purposes, such as a religious cultural hall, feel that it is necessary to transform their surroundings to something more wedding-like. Still, other couples who have selected a theme for their wedding activities, go all out to decorate the reception site.

The decorations may include anything from antique furniture for a Victorian wedding to hay wagons in which to put the gifts at an outdoor barbecue. What you need to remember when selecting decorations for the reception site are the timetable of events, how much time is available to actually place the decorations, the style of your wedding, how the decorations can continue the theme and color, and your budget. Decorations can be expensive if the area is large or specific items are needed.

—Music and Musicians—

Music is one way to set a definite mood at your reception and emphasize special moments. The music might be festive, romantic, light-hearted, or from a specific period. Musical selections are somewhat dictated by the style of your wedding but should also reflect your personal preferences as well as those of your guests.

If your budget will allow, you will want to plan for background music while you are standing in the receiving line and during dinner. If you are not having dance music, these selections could be played by a pianist, a harpist, or a small combo. If you have dancing, a band can play both sets with the dance music usually beginning shortly after the meal has been cleared.

When hiring musicians to play dance music, remember to select both musicians and music that are easy to dance to, that appeal to guests of all ages, and that are familiar. It is acceptable to make a list of songs you would like to have played and make certain the band will take requests from the guests.

If live musicians are too expensive, a popular alternative is to have pre-recorded music with a disc jockey who acts as the master of ceremonies and takes requests from the guests.

❖ To select the musicians, you may want to try one of the following:

- Ask friends or family members.
- Scout college musical performances.
- Ask a professional referral service, musicians union, or other established performance groups.
- Attend local nightclubs and listen to the groups performing.

❖ After you have selected three possibilities, follow these guidelines:

1. Find out where each group of musicians is playing and go listen to them perform before you make an appointment to speak with them.

2. If you like what you hear, make an appointment to discuss details and prices.

3. Find out how many are in the group and what musical instruments are available.

4. Are they willing to play the music you request and, if they do not know a specific, important song, will they learn it? Ask for their suggestions; if they are accustomed to playing weddings, they may know what works well and what does not.

   If you make special requests and they do not have the music, are you required to purchase it for them or will they take care of it and cover the costs in their fees?

5. Find out how they calculate their charges and what their fees are. Do they charge by the hour or do they charge a flat, daily fee–in which case, are their hours flexible or do they charge overtime fees? Find out how they bill for partial hours, and how many and how long their breaks are.

6. Do they require any special equipment and, if so, do they supply it or are you required to?

7. Make certain everyone understands how the musicians are to be dressed. It is important that you are considerate of the wardrobe they have. If you feel strongly that they wear something specific or unusual, you may be required to pay for the purchase or rental of the garments.

8. Discuss any specific events that are scheduled in which you may want the bandleader to act as master of ceremonies or in which you wish the band to participate. For example, do you want a special song played for the first dance, the last dance, or during the garter ceremony? Give the bandleader a detailed itinerary and a list of songs to play and when so no cues are misunderstood.

9. Make certain the person in charge of the group will agree to visit the reception site at least two weeks ahead of time to insure that all details are attended to. For example, are there enough electrical outlets? Is there

and cropping. Do they use special techniques such as soft focus lenses, multiple exposures, or split framing?

As well as inspecting their portfolio, study their personality. You want to select someone who has a pleasant personality, someone who will listen to what you want, and someone with whom you are comfortable. Some wedding photographers can be overbearing in their demands and offensive to guests and wedding party participants.

3. Show him/her photographs that you have cut out of magazines and books that depict the look you want.

4. Inquire as to their wedding packages and what is included. Most will have a brochure describing their service, policies, and packaged price sheets. Are the pictures they have selected to include in the package the ones you really want? How much is the charge for additional pictures? Make certain you compare this price to the price that would be charged if you had all of the photographs taken that you want? What is the charge for additional photographs that will be wanted by you and other family members or wedding participants?

5. Discuss other possible photographs with the photographer. For example, a pre-wedding picture of you to display at the reception, a

photograph of you and the groom to include on your wedding invitation or thank-you notes, or a special photograph to give as a gift to parents or participants.

6. Most photographers who specialize in weddings concentrate on typical wedding photographs. If you want something out of the ordinary, you may not want to hire a wedding specialist but a commercial photographer to achieve your desires. This author finds that "wedding photographers" cannot seem to grasp the concept of unposed photographs of guests at a wedding, of a picture of you and your attendants doing something other than standing in a straight line, or of you and the groom cropped in such a way that may not be as traditional as they are accustomed to. They seem to know only one way—the traditional way!

7. Make certain the photographer visits both the ceremony and reception sites with you to check on the logistics. Discuss any restrictions for taking photographs during certain times in certain locations.

8. Review the times of the ceremony and the reception and the locations (indoors or outdoors can make a great deal of difference to a photographer).

9. Discuss the attire he/she will wear to the wedding so that it is in keeping with the other participants.

10. Make certain that the photographer you speak with will be the one who actually takes all of the photographs before and during your wedding and he/she will not turn the actual work over to a less-experienced employee.

11. Discuss with the photographer who actually owns the film and the proofs of the pictures taken for you. Some photographers will not give you the film to have processed elsewhere. They own it and they develop it.

12. Discuss his/her fee. Is there a separate charge for time and travel to come to the ceremony and reception site to take the photos?

13. What kind of a deposit is required? Make certain you place your deposit on a credit card, protecting yourself by special consumer protection laws should something go wrong with the photographs you had agreed to.

14. What is his/her cancellation policy?

15. Make certain you have a detailed contract with your photographer that states times; dates; number and kinds of photographs to be taken; as well as all charges for time, travel, and photos.

PHOTOGRAPHER'S CHECKLIST

Photographer_____

Address_____

Phone_____

Arrival Time_____

Departure Time_____

Photos before the Ceremony_____

_____

_____

_____

Photos during the Ceremony_____

_____

_____

_____

Photos after the Ceremony_____

_____

_____

_____

Photos during the Reception_____

_____

_____

Package Contents_____

_____ _____

_____

_____

_____ _____

_____

Package Price_____

_____

Prices per Additional Photo_____

_____

Additional Charges_____

_____

_____

Ownership of Film and Proofs_____

_____

Total Price_____

_____

Deposit Date and Amount _____

_____

Balance Amount and Due Date_____

_____

Videographer

Videotaping is the newest fashion in wedding memories and, due to modern technology, promises to become as much of a tradition as taking photographs. It is this author's suggestion that this be one place that you do not skimp on costs. The tape of your wedding, if correctly and professionally done, will be played over and over for years to come. It will be the only actual record of what was said, who attended, and who did what. For my own wedding, I did not think this was as important as it was, so I had the taping done by a relative and it is the one aspect of the entire wedding festivities that I wish I could redo. Regardless of a friend's or relative's intent, only a professional can give you the quality of taping, the thoroughness that comes from experience, and the memories that will be able to watch for generations to come.

Once you have selected your ceremony and reception sites, you can begin interviewing videotaping companies. Use the same sources that you did for selecting a photographer.

❖ **Once you have selected three possible candidates, follow the guidelines listed below:**

1. Make an appointment with each and allow one hour to discuss the details. Make certain he/she shows you his/her operation and equipment.

2. Ask to see tapes of weddings previously recorded and for a description of the proposed agenda for your taping.

3. Ask for references and inspect the kind of equipment that will be used. Ask if he/she uses an assistant.

4. Discuss the type of production you want. Can he/she work with the photographer? Can music be dubbed into the tape? Will the film be edited? If the film is edited, will he/she give you the raw footage? (Some of the funniest moments may end up on the cutting room floor if you do not rescue them.) Because this is such a new area, make certain to ask for his/her suggestions and recommendations.

5. Make certain he/she visits the actual ceremony and reception site prior to the date to check for any obstacles to and restrictions on videotaping.

6. Discuss his/her attire at the wedding festivities so he/she is dressed similar to other participants.

7. Discuss his/her fee. Does he/she charge a flat fee or by the hour? What is the additional charge for editing, dubbing, and other features? Is there a travel fee and overtime charge if he/she is required to stay longer than expected? What deposit is required? What is his/her cancellation policy? Does he/she guarantee the quality of his/her work?

8. Receive a written contract stating the date, the times, the place, and an explanation of videography expected.

9. Again, put your deposit on a credit card, protecting yourself as much as possible if the film does not turn out.

VIDEOTAPE CHECKLIST

You will want to adapt and complete this worksheet and give it to the videographer so that he/she has a detailed worksheet of what is expected and when.

Name_____

Address_____

Phone_____

Arrival Time_____

Events to Videotape_____

_____

_____

Departure Time_____

Videotaping Service_____

Editing_____

Sound Dubbing_____

Special Effects_____

Miscellaneous_____ _____

_____

_____

_____

_____

_____

Additional Tapes_____

Cost per Tape_____

Date Video Will Be Ready_____

Total Cost_____

Deposit_____

Balance_____

Other_____

_____

_____

_____

_____

_____

Tipping

Tipping is often confusing in relation to reception services. Nonetheless, there will be a number of persons you will want to tip because of a job so well done. Below is a brief guideline, but you should feel free to use your best judgment. As a rule, photographers, bakers, florists, and musicians are not tipped unless they provide exceptional service or special help with the reception. It is generally the male host of the reception or the best man who tips for the services.

Food Service/Hotel/Restaurant

A 15% to 20% tip on the reception bill is divided among waiters, waitresses, bartenders, and others. At your discretion, you may wish to tip appropriate amounts to others who have also done an exceptionally good job, such as the caterer, hotel banquet manager, wedding coordinator, and site manager.

Hotel/Restaurant/Hall Attendants

Plan to tip 50¢ per guest or a prearranged sum to the coat room attendant and powder room attendant.

Drivers

Plan to tip 15% to 20% of transportation costs.

Traditional Activities

As archaic as it may sound to a modern bride, traditional activities still have a place at the reception. Throwing the bride's bouquet to see who will be next to marry is fun for all of the guests!

The sequence of reception events might be as follows:

- Guests arrive and sign the guest book.
- Guests give gifts to person in charge of gifts.
- Guests enter the receiving line.
- Guests mingle and are served hors d'oeuvres and cocktails.
- Guests are officially seated.
- Bride, groom, and wedding party are announced.
- Blessing by the officiant.
- Toast by the best man, followed by other toasts.
- Food service begins.
- Newlyweds' first dance with other dances following.
- Dessert is served.
- The cake is cut.
- Throwing of the bouquet and garter.
- Newlyweds' farewell dance.
- Departure.

Guest Book

The guest book is usually on a decorated table near the entrance to the reception. You may elect to have a guest book attendant who encourages guests to sign their names and add their wishes for you and the groom. This is a wonderful memento to read after the wedding and should not be overlooked as part of the reception activities.

Gift Table

The gifts are displayed unopened on a special table, usually arranged with a few special gifts that were delivered and opened before the wedding. For example, you may want to show off your china, crystal, silver and, perhaps, an heirloom quilt.

Receiving Line

The receiving line is a traditional part of the wedding reception and is a way for guests to meet you, the groom, the wedding party participants, and both sets of parents. It is the perfect opportunity for you to thank everyone for coming and to introduce new family members and friends to one another. A nice touch to any receiving line is to have someone stationed at the end of it with a tray of glasses filled with champagne or other refreshments to offer to the guests as they leave the line and enter the reception. If your guest list is large and the receiving line is anticipated to be very long, eliminate the attendants, have waiters mingle among the guests in line with trays of hors d'oeuvres and drinks, and provide soft background music.

Since the receiving line is the beginning of the reception, do not schedule formal picture taking directly before the receiving line is to congregate. If guests are arriving while you are having pictures taken, it can cause many unnecessary delays.

Your father traditionally acts as host and mingles with the guests while the rest of the wedding party is standing in the receiving line. Your mother heads the line. If your father decides to participate in the line, he is next. Next to him is the groom's mother, then the groom's father (if one father participates, both should), then you and the groom, followed by the maid/matron-of-honor and the bridesmaids. Child attendants do not participate and, traditionally, neither do the groomsmen. Today's brides, however, oftentimes elect to include the groomsmen or change the order of the receiving line to fit their own personal needs. Any changes have become an accepted way of adapting traditional guidelines to fit personal desires. If the line is too long, then the bridesmaids and ushers may be asked to mingle with the guests.

At a very large, formal wedding, you may elect to have an announcer stand next to your mother and announce each guest to her.

When orchestrating the receiving line, if either set of parents is divorced and/or remarried, you will need to consider everyone's feelings, who is paying for the wedding, who raised you or the groom, and how well all of the ex-spouses and stepfamily members get along. Several different alternatives will work for who stands by whom in the line, depending on the above considerations. Take the traditional outline of who stands where and adjust it to fit your individual needs. In today's society, there really is no right or wrong way. In fact, many brides are electing to have no receiving line at all but instead place themselves and the groom in one strategic location for the majority of the evening where guests can easily find them and talk to them without someone waiting behind them.

❖ Hints for standing in a receiving line

- You and the groom should go over the guest list the day before the wedding to familiarize yourselves with the names as much as possible.

- All wedding participants who stand in line should remove their gloves.

- If you are worried about perspiring palms, lightly apply an antiperspirant to your hands.

- You might hold your bouquet in your left hand or set it aside while standing in line. The bridesmaids keep their flowers in their left hands as well.

- Introduce yourself first to all guests you do not know.

- When introducing guests to the person next in line, give their name and who they are associated with in the wedding party.

- Limit your conversations so as to keep the line moving as quickly as possible.

- When the majority of guests have arrived, the line disperses.

After the receiving line, it is traditional to allow the guests and the wedding participants to mingle and chat. This is an excellent time to have the photographer take some of your pictures or candid shots.

The only thing to do is to hug one's friend tight...
Edith Wharton

Seating

The wedding reception host announces (or has the bandleader announce) that it is time to be seated for dinner. An organized seating plan will expedite this process even though you do not want your guests to feel rushed. For assigned seats, you will need place cards to be printed which should be arranged in alphabetical order on a table near the entrance to the reception site. The place cards will have the guest's name and the table number at which he/she is to be seated.

❖ **Traditional seating arrangements are as follows:**

The Bride's Table

This table may be of any shape and may be placed wherever in the room that is most strategic (at the end of a long room, in the middle of the room, or on an elevated platform) for all of the guests to see you and the groom. Unless the table is round, seating is on one side only so the guests' view is not obstructed. You and the groom sit in the center of the table; your honor attendant sits on the groom's left, with the best man seated on your right. The bridesmaids and ushers are then alternated around the table. Attendants who are married to each other sit together.

Traditionally, place cards mark each seat at the bride's table and parents' table but are optional elsewhere.

The Parents' Table

Unless the table is round, your mother and father sit in the honored places for hosts at opposite ends. The groom's father sits at your mother's right, the wedding officiant at her left, the groom's mother at your father's right, the wedding officiant's spouse at his left. If you wish to arrange two parents' tables, you may do so with honored guests from each family seated in an honored position with the parents.

If any set of parents is divorced, seat them at different tables of honor and surround them with family and friends.

Additional Tables

If you plan on having prearranged seating, then each table will have a number placed in the center of the table. The place cards at the entrance will be used by the guests to find their assigned table. Once the guests reach their table, they may or may not have place cards on their napkins or on top of the plates to tell them which actual seat is theirs. If there are place cards, the names are written in their most simplified form, for example: Nancy Whitley or Mrs. Whitley, never Mrs. George J. Whitley.

Special Children's Table

If you have included several children on your guest list, it is often nice to have a special table with a specific chaperon for them. You may wish to include additional items, such as coloring books, for them to use to entertain themselves while the adults have a leisurely meal.

_____ Personal Touches _____

Individualizing your wedding within the bounds of tradition and style makes the event even more meaningful. You and your fiancé may want to include some of these ideas:

✦ After all of the guests have been seated, the host traditionally introduces you and the groom by saying something like "May I give to you— for the first time—Mr. and Mrs. Ronald J. Tribe." This announcement may be accompanied by a fanfare or drumroll from the band, if you wish. You and the groom enter from a doorway as the announcement is made or stand if you are seated.

✦ The host then announces the members of the wedding party individually, if seated. Or if the party enters through a doorway, each brides-maid is escorted by a groomsman and her name is announced first.

✦ The officiant of the wedding ceremony, if he attends, or an honored guest is invited to bless the meal and the couple as they begin their new life together. This needs to be prearranged so that someone is not called on unexpectedly and is uncomfortable in doing so. This prayer should be in keeping with the religious beliefs of the officiant who performed the ceremony.

✦ Before the meal is about to be served, it is appropriate for the best man to propose a toast to you and the groom. He talks of how you both met and a few words about the hopes the two of you have for the future. At the end of the toast, he raises his glass and toasts to you. All guests raise their glasses and join the toast. You place your arm through the groom's and you both drink. The locking of arms signifies the intertwining of your new lives. The groom may then respond by thanking the best man and toasting the bride, his new in-laws, and his parents. You then add your own toast honoring the groom and his family and thanking your parents. (For ideas on what to say, see *Toasts & Speeches* by Jo Packham.)

✦ After you and the groom have finished your meal, the two of you take the dance floor and dance the first dance. The bandleader announces the song which has been prearranged because of its special meaning to the two of you.

✦ This dance is followed by your dance with your father while the groom dances with your mother. After that, the order is as follows: the groom's father dances with you and the groom with his mother; next you dance with the best man and the groom dances with the maid/ matron-of-honor; then the groom dances with all of the female attendants and you with all of the male attendants; the attendants then dance with each other.

✦ About the time you begin dancing with the best man, the bandleader should announce for all of the guests to begin dancing.

✦ After all of the special dances, the cutting of the cake ceremony begins. This is approximately 30 minutes after the meal, if there is a formal, sit-down dinner with dancing; if not, it is traditional to have this ritual take place approximately one hour after the receiving line ends.

✦ For the cutting of the cake ceremony, you place your hand on the knife and the groom places his hand over yours as the cake is cut. The groom then takes the first piece and feeds part of it to you, after which you do the same. This symbolizes the sharing you will be doing the rest of your lives. A loving gesture that is becoming tradition is for you to give your new in-laws their pieces after that; then the groom serves your parents next. The remainder of the cake is then cut and served to the guests.

✦ Another ritual that is a long-standing tradition at weddings is the throwing of the bouquet. You will want to have a smaller bouquet made especially for this moment; that way the recipient can keep the bouquet as a memento. This usually occurs approximately one-half hour before your planned departure. The bandleader announces the event. All of the unmarried females gather behind you, as you toss your bouquet over your shoulder. The person who catches the bouquet is considered lucky and the next to marry.

✦ Next comes the throwing of the garter (or this may come before the throwing of the bouquet, if you prefer). As in the bouquet throwing tradition, all of the unmarried males are asked to gather round. You are seated, with the groom standing next to you. With fanfare from the band, he removes your garter and tosses it over his shoulder to the waiting crowd. Oftentimes, the garter is the "something blue" that you have worn to the wedding. The lucky recipient is also the next in line to marry.

✦ With the reception drawing to a close, it is time to make your departure. You will want to retire to the dressing rooms and change into your going-away clothes. You are usually escorted by your mother and bridesmaids. The groom is accompanied by his best man. As soon as you are ready, you join the groom and have the remaining parents escorted to your room to say your good-byes and thank-yous.

✦ Before you leave, however, you may wish to dance the final farewell dance, at which time all other guests leave the floor. You then make your grand exit with guests throwing rice and extending good wishes as you bring to a close one of the happiest days of your life!

Index

4029